AMPHIBIANS
Water-to-Land Animals

by Laura Purdie Salas

illustrated by Kristin Kest

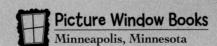

Picture Window Books
Minneapolis, Minnesota

Thanks to our advisers for their expertise, research, and advice:

Robert C. Dowler, Ph.D.
Tippett Professor of Biology
Angelo State University
San Angelo, Texas

Terry Flaherty, Ph.D., Professor of English
Minnesota State University, Mankato

Editor: Shelly Lyons
Designer: Lori Bye
Page Production: Melissa Kes
Art Director: Nathan Gassman
Editorial Director: Nick Healy
Creative Director: Joe Ewest
The illustrations in this book were created digitally.

Picture Window Books
151 Good Counsel Drive
P.O. Box 669
Mankato, MN 56002-0669
877-845-8392
www.picturewindowbooks.com

Photo Credits: page 22 (top row, left to right, and repeated uses),
Shutterstock/Paul-André Belle-Isle; iStockphoto/Carolina K. Smith;
iStockphoto/John Bell; iStockphoto/Eric Isselée; Shutterstock/Carsten
Reisinger; iStockphoto/George Peters; iStockphoto/Eric Isselée;
Shutterstock/Steffen Foerster Photography; Shutterstock/Gregg Williams;
iStockphoto/Le Do.

Printed in the United States of America.

All books published by Picture Window Books
are manufactured with paper containing at least
10 percent post-consumer waste.

Library of Congress Cataloging-in-Publication Data
Salas, Laura Purdie.
Amphibians : water-to-land animals / by Laura Purdie Salas ;
illustrated by Kristin Kest.
p. cm. — (Amazing science. Animal classification)
Includes index.
ISBN 978-1-4048-5521-2 (library binding)
1. Amphibians—Classification—Juvenile literature.
2. Amphibians—Juvenile literature. I. Kest, Kristin, ill. II. Title.
QL645.S25 2010
597.8—dc22
2009003290

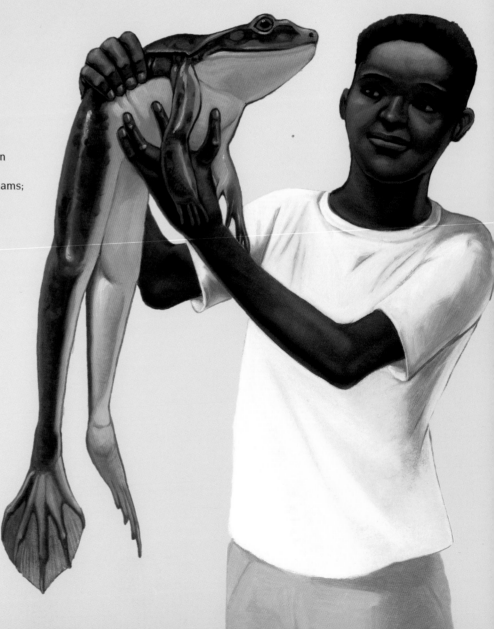

Table of Contents

A World Full of Animals

Millions of animals live on our planet. Scientists classify animals, or group them together, by looking at how the animals are alike or different.

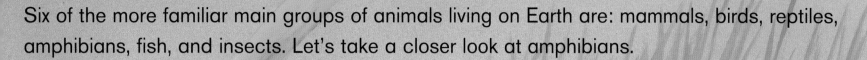

Six of the more familiar main groups of animals living on Earth are: mammals, birds, reptiles, amphibians, fish, and insects. Let's take a closer look at amphibians.

The study of amphibians and reptiles is called herpetology. There are more than 6,000 species of amphibians on Earth. New ones are being found all the time.

How Do You Know It's an Amphibian?

All amphibians have certain things in common. First, they are all vertebrates. That means they have a backbone. Amphibians are also cold-blooded. Their body temperature changes with their surroundings. They must lie in the sunlight to warm their bodies. Most amphibians have smooth skin that's a bit wet.

desert slender salamander

Many amphibians spend part of their lives in water and part of their lives on land. They start out in a freshwater pond or stream. As they grow, they move onto land.

tadpoles

Amphibians first lived on Earth about 360 million years ago. They were around long before dinosaurs!

Two Groups of Amphibians

There are three basic groups of amphibians. The largest group is frogs and toads. They have chubby bodies and four legs. Their long back legs help them jump. Frogs live in or near water and have skin that feels somewhat wet. Toads also live near water but have drier skin.

green frogs

Salamanders and newts are another group. They have long bodies, four legs, and tails. They have short, weak legs and move slowly. Salamanders have smooth, wet skin. They look a lot like lizards. But lizards have dry, scaly skin. Newts have rough, drier skin.

northern red salamander

A Third Group of Amphibians

The last group of amphibians is called caecilians. Lots of people have never heard of them. They look like giant earthworms, but they have sharp teeth. They live in very warm areas, often deep underground or in the water. They come above ground when conditions are wet.

caecilians

Caecilians have very small eyes and no ears. They have tiny tentacles between their nose and eyes. The tentacles help them find their way underground.

The Big Change

Most amphibians hatch from eggs in a pond. They do not look like their mother or father. They have a completely different shape. Frogs and toads, for instance, hatch from eggs as tadpoles.

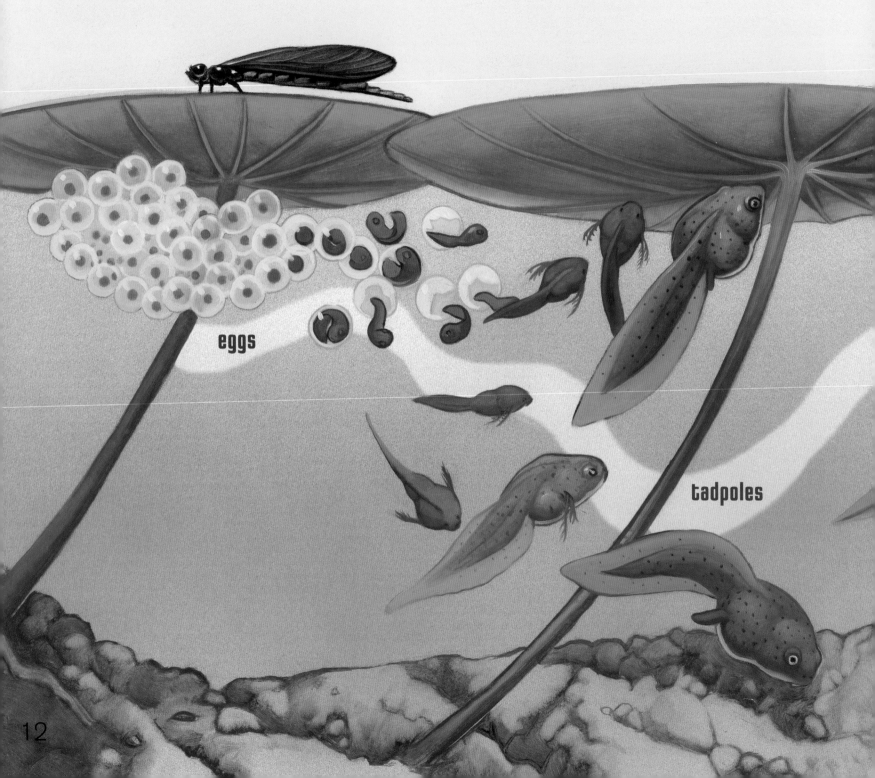

eggs

tadpoles

Young amphibians swim in the water. For a few days, they breathe through gills. Then they grow legs and lungs. When the young amphibians finish changing, they look like their parents.

adult frog

juvenile frog

Lungs are not the only organ adult amphibians use to breathe. They also take in oxygen through their skin!

13

Where Do Amphibians Live?

Amphibians live all around the world. The only place they aren't found is Antarctica. But all amphibians must have moisture. Many of them live in tropical rain forests. They often live in marshes near lakes or rivers.

central newt

giant toad

caecilian

tree frog

spotted salamander

Some amphibians, such as the water-holding frog, can survive in areas that have dry periods. This frog must dig itself underground. It keeps itself wet by producing a slimy layer on its skin.

15

What's for Dinner?

As adults, amphibians are carnivores, or meat-eaters. They eat bugs, snails, worms, and spiders. Large amphibians, such as giant toads, even eat small mammals, birds, and frogs. Frogs and toads have sticky tongues to help them catch food. Salamanders and caecilians catch very slow-moving animals, such as worms and slugs.

giant marine toad

16

leopard frog

As amphibians grow, their skin gets too tight. Several times a year, they form a new skin, and the old skin peels off. When amphibians shed their skin, they often eat it!

Unusual Amphibians

Some amphibians do amazing things. The eggs of the Suriname female toad stick to its back. Then the eggs sink into the mother's skin, and the skin grows around them. When the young toads hatch from their eggs, they pop right out of their mother's back.

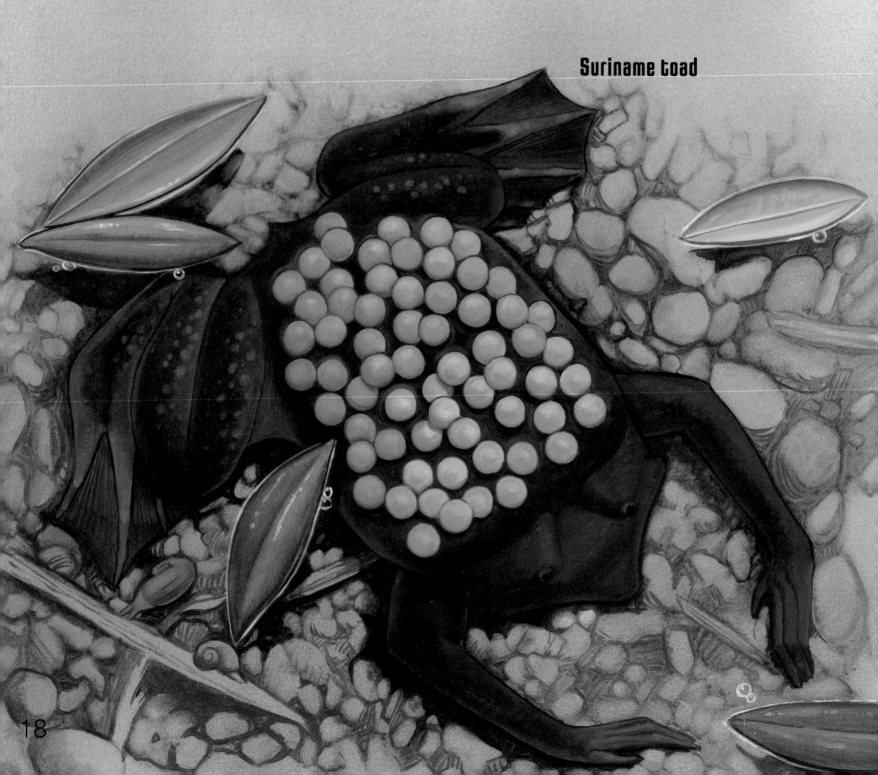

Suriname toad

Arboreal salamanders and frogs climb trees. Their large toe pads help them grip branches. The Wallace's frog even flies—kind of. Using giant stretches of skin between its fingers and toes, the frog glides from one tree to another.

arboreal salamander

Amphibians in Our World

Amphibians have lived on Earth for around 360 million years. But many amphibian species, such as the Goliath frog and the Chinese giant salamander, are in danger of dying out. Scientists think weather changes and pollution are two reasons. Also, many amphibians have no place to live. That happens when people cut down forests and drain wetlands to put up more buildings.

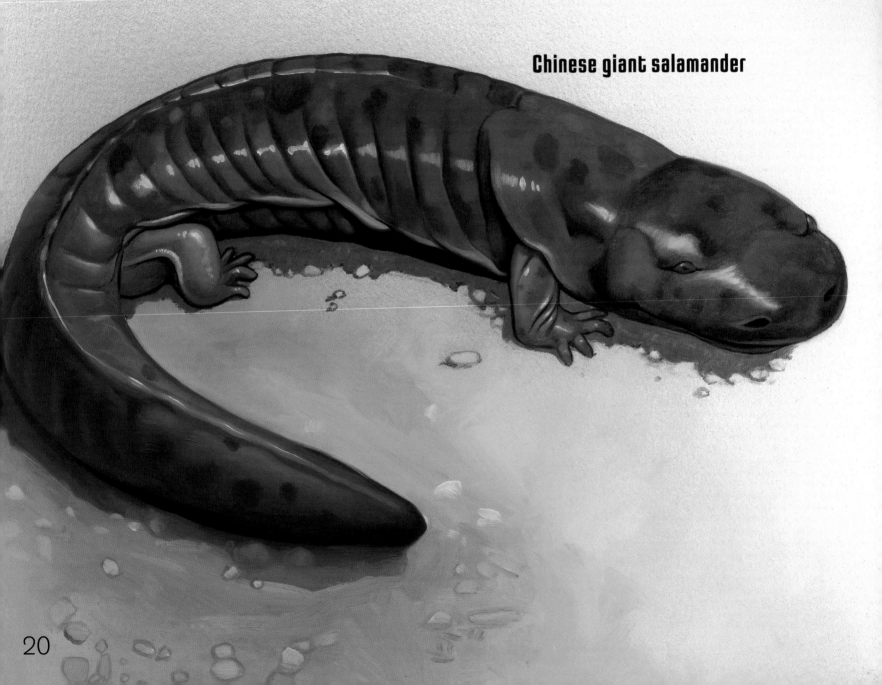

Chinese giant salamander

Healthy amphibians show us we have a healthy planet. We can find better ways to live with these wonderful animals.

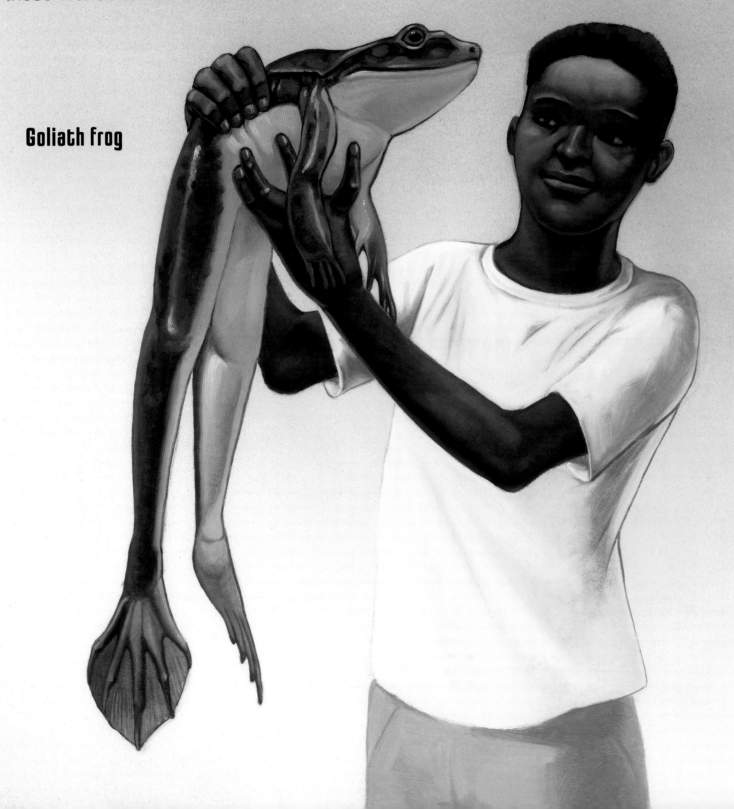

Goliath frog

Scientific Classification Chart

The animal classification system used today was created by Carolus Linnaeus. The system works by sorting animals based on how they are alike or different.

All living things are first put into a kingdom. There are five main kingdoms. Then they are also assigned to groups within six other main headings. The headings are: phylum, class, order, family, genus, and species.

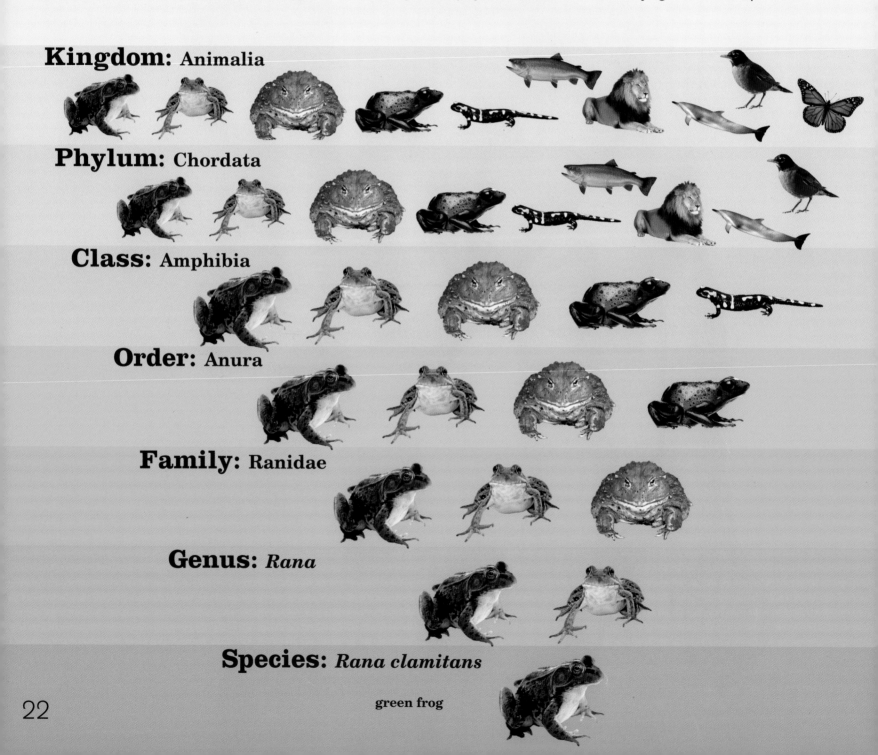

Kingdom: Animalia

Phylum: Chordata

Class: Amphibia

Order: Anura

Family: Ranidae

Genus: *Rana*

Species: *Rana clamitans*

green frog

Extreme Amphibians

Largest amphibian: The Chinese giant salamander grows to 6 feet (1.8 meters) and 140 pounds (63 kilograms)!

Smallest amphibian: One of the smallest amphibians is the Izecksohn's toad. It is so lightweight that five of them together weigh less than 1 ounce (28 grams)! It is less than 0.4 inches (1 centimeter) long.

Most poisonous frog: The golden dart frog has enough poison to kill 10 humans!

Biggest frog: The Goliath frog grows to a whopping 6 to 7.2 pounds (2.7 to 3.2 kg) and 8 to 12 inches (20.3 to 30.5 cm) in length.

Longest-lived amphibian: The Japanese giant salamander lives the longest of any amphibian. Some Japanese giant salamanders living in zoos have survived to be 55 years old.

Glossary

amphibians—animals that are vertebrates, are cold-blooded, and have smooth skin that's a bit wet

arboreal—living in trees

carnivore—a meat-eating animal

cold-blooded—having a body temperature that changes with the surroundings

gills—part of a tadpole or fish that helps it breathe underwater

herpetology—the study of amphibians and reptiles

lungs—the organs in the chest that help some animals breathe

mammals—animals that have a backbone, have hair or fur, feed their young milk, are warm-blooded, and have lungs that take in oxygen

oxygen—a gas that people and animals must breathe to stay alive

pollution—dirty, smelly waste that makes air and water dangerous to living things

reptiles—animals that are vertebrates, have scales, are cold-blooded, have lungs, and (usually) lay eggs

species—a specific type of animal that has certain characteristics

vertebrate—an animal that has a backbone

wetlands—an area that has very wet soil, tall marsh grasses, and often shallow water

To Learn More

More Books to Read

Clarke, Barry. *Amphibian*. New York: DK Pub., 2005.

Kalman, Bobbie. *Frogs and Other Amphibians*. New York: Crabtree Pub. Co., 2005.

Slade, Suzanne. *From Tadpole to Frog: Following the Life Cycle*. Mankato, Minn.: Picture Window Books, 2008.

Internet Sites

FactHound offers a safe, fun way to find Internet sites related to this book. All of the sites on FactHound have been researched by our staff.

Here's all you do:

Visit *www.facthound.com*

FactHound will fetch the best sites for you!

Index

Look for all of the books in the Amazing Science: Animal Classification series:

Amphibians: Water-to-Land Animals

Birds: Winged and Feathered Animals

Fish: Finned and Gilled Animals

Insects: Six-Legged Animals

Mammals: Hairy, Milk-Making Animals

Reptiles: Scaly-Skinned Animals